Just The Basics

Simple Help for Starting a Business and Creating a Good Bookkeeping System

By Denise Cotè

Table of Contents

INTRODUCTION

This is a guide to help you choose a business structure and give you a basic course in some simple bookkeeping principles for your small business. I have been a bookkeeper for various small businesses for over 30 years. I have degrees in Accounting, Business Administration, and Marketing. I also have my own business and it is called SOHO Bookkeeping & Support, Inc. SOHO is an acronym for "Small Office, Home Office". I presently work with 15 companies. These are all different types of businesses, industries, company sizes, and structures. The one thing that they all have in common is they all need a business structure and an easy bookkeeping system. Every business needs this. Your business needs this because you want to be able to plan for growth, and make well thought out decisions as you take your business into the future.

I first thought of writing this book when I realized all of my customers were asking me the same questions about their business structures and bookkeeping systems. One of the goals in *my* business is to help customers feel more secure about where their money is going to, or coming from. Generally, by the time someone calls me to help them with their books, they've waited a little too long and there are some messes to clear up. In all of these cases it is NOT because the owner of the business could care less about their livelihood, or if their bills get paid or if the IRS comes knocking on their door. It is simply because they just don't know the differences between the basic business structures and a few simple bookkeeping principles.

My customers are tops in their fields. They are experts at doing what they do best, which is why they started their own businesses in the first place. Most of the businesses I work with admittedly do not know much about the how's or why's of their business structures or their bookkeeping systems.

Take for example bookkeeping systems. They are all based on the same accounting principles. What I want to accomplish with this book is for you, the business owner or potential business owner, to become confident and comfortable with the idea that, if you want to, you can compare the basic types of business structures, and you can set up and maintain your own set of books for your own company. Or, if you would rather hire someone to do the bookkeeping for your business, you will know what they are doing and will be able to actively participate in these important areas of your company.

This book is not going to give you any insight on tax laws or legal issues. I am not a Lawyer or a Certified Public Accountant. If you have questions for either of these professions, you should consult a Lawyer or a CPA. What this book will do is give you some very simple explanations on the basic business structures and how to set up and maintain your own set of books for your company. This will make things go smoothly if or when the time does come for you to consult a Lawyer or your CPA, especially at tax time.

Someone wise once told me true peace of mind is not merely the absence of conflict but the ability to cope with it. So remember, keep it simple and good luck to you in your business!

Yay! You Made The Choice!

Making the choice to start up your own business is probably the hardest decision of the whole process. It is a wonderful feeling to be able to give yourself that much independence in that portion of your life. Most people think they can't go into business until they have enough money set aside. Or they can't do it until they can make a total commitment, to be able to do their own business on a full time basis. So by now, you probably have figured out that neither of these is true. I believe that just having the drive, enthusiasm and the talent are enough to start up your own business. The rest will follow. If you have to "keep your day job" and do your own business part time for a while, that's just fine. If you don't have enough money just yet start your process anyways. In doing so you may find ways to fund yourself you hadn't thought of if you had never begun. In other words, it can be done if you really want to do it.

That said, the next decision is what kind of business structure should you choose? That's a decision that you should make after educating yourself on each of the different basic styles. Many people pay their lawyers or CPAs to make that choice for them.

I think this actually is advisable *if you are going into business with a partner or partners*. By all means have a professional help you choose the best structure and put everything in writing so there will be no question at all as to how each partner is affected by the business. Do this even if your partner is your spouse or a family member. I'm so serious. You will be glad you did.

Otherwise, if you are just doing your business venture on your own, congratulations, you are an independent entrepreneur! And, chances are you can choose and set up your business on your own with the aid of the internet and without paying a lawyer or your CPA.

In doing this, please keep in mind that all the information you find on the internet or otherwise about the various basic business structures, as in this guide, are for educational purposes only. If you do feel you need legal advice or the aid of your CPA, then Please Do Contact These Professions For Help! There is a lot of really good information on the website for the Internal Revenue Service, (irs.gov), and also, please consult your state's Secretary of State, Department of Revenue, and Department of Licensing sites. In our state, the state of Washington, these sites and departments are separate. These sites are all filled with a wealth of information. And you can also use these websites to register your business, file the required forms, and pay the necessary fees for your chosen business structure.

The Basic Business Structures

The basic small business structures are a Sole Proprietorship, Incorporation, particularly an S Corp, an LLC, and a Nonprofit Corporation. First, look at a Sole Proprietorship:

Sole Proprietorship

In a Sole Proprietorship you are your business and your business is you. It doesn't really matter if you have a separate checking account, although that helps. All your expenses and income from your personal life or your business life are all one. Likewise if anyone decides to sue you your personal property can be affected. And if you have a family this could, in turn affect their property too. Along this line, if you are married your spouse could also responsible for any profits or debts as well. A Sole Proprietorship can be formed anywhere your business is located. And its duration can be for the lifetime of the individual in whose name it's registered.

If you decide to have employees, I would suggest getting an employer identification number from the Internal Revenue Service. You can do this by going to the website of irs.gov, download the form SS-4, and you can fill this out and submit it online. It costs nothing and they will email you back your new employer identification number within the hour. As a Sole Proprietor you can also just use your social security number for all your tax forms but in this day and age it is highly unadvisable.

It is likely your state has a state tax identification number for businesses. Plus you will want to register your business name with your state and make sure no one else is using that same business name. You can go to your state's Secretary of State website for this and at least that will be the good place to start. You will need this state number if you are planning to sell any retail items, meaning you will be charging and collecting sales tax. You will also need it if you are providing services, or anything that will bring income to you that will eventually become reportable to your state. You will also need your state's identification number if you are planning to have employees. This will identify you to your state on any state payroll tax forms such as unemployment or workman's compensation. More on this in the bookkeeping section of this guide!

Also, you will need to buy a license to do business from the city or town you live in. Maybe your town has its own website where you can do this. Or you can just go to your city's business offices and buy one. This should probably be done after you register with your state and get your state identification number. You may need that information before registering with your city. Some cities and towns are set up so that their individual business licenses are bought when you register and pay for your state's fees. When checking with the city or town where your place of business is located consider the fact that you may also be doing business in the surrounding cities or towns and you may also need business licenses for those as well. When visiting your city's offices consider joining your chamber of commerce. Do this especially if you like networking and general schmoozing. It's all good for business!

As a Sole Proprietor you can just take draws from your company. Draws DO NOT affect the net profit of your company. (Your Net Profit is your very bottom line. There is more about this in the bookkeeping section of this guide.) Or you can pay yourself as an employee. You can do both if you like. Paychecks DO affect the net profit of your company. As an employee you will take at least social security and medicare out of your paycheck and your company matches the amounts just like with the rest of your employees. This rate is 7.65% for each the employer and the employee for both social security and medicare combined. This is one way to reduce the net profit of your company when tax time comes. As a Sole Proprietor you also get to pay a Self Employment Tax on the net profit at tax time. Self Employment Tax is the way the self-employed sole proprietor pays into social security and medicare. The current rate for Self Employment Tax is 15.3%. The IRS gives a 50% discount on this. So you see, if this isn't too confusing, that you will pay the full rate of the combined social security and medicare tax (15.3% for the employer and employee parts), if you take a paycheck. Or you can pay 50% of the 15.3% self employment tax on your net profit. Or you can do both. One way or another you will be paying into your social security and medicare.

As you can see there are choices in regards to taking your pay from your company. As with any new business you will need to see what will be the best solution for you. If you decide to be a Sole Proprietor you can try different ways and see what works best for you at tax time. And speaking of tax time, as a Sole Proprietor you are required to file your taxes by April 15th just like all U.S. individuals, because as a Sole Proprietor your business taxes are your personal taxes.

Incorporation and S Corp Designation

Incorporation is a possibility for any size company. Some people think you have to be a large company to be a corporation. But you can be incorporated even if you are just one person. I operate my business as an S Corp. We can look at more on that designation in a moment.

It is pretty easy to incorporate. Incorporating is done on a state level. So for instance in my state, Washington, I start by going online to the WA Secretary of State website. I can apply online and at this writing is costs $195. And any time from immediately to a couple days I get a new state identification number for my business and the date of my incorporation confirmed by the state of WA.

Next, if I didn't already have one, I go online to the IRS at irs.gov and fill in and submit online a Form SS-4 for a new employer identification number. This is free and they will email the number they have assigned to me probably within the hour.

Now with my new state identification number, my date of incorporation, and my new IRS employer identification number I go to my state's Department of Licensing website. Here I fill in and submit online my application for my new business license in the state of Washington. At this writing this costs $59. Really, surprisingly it is this easy.

In a corporation there is a board of directors, stockholders, and employees. These can be anybody. Even one person, like you! They can be people you know, people interested in investing in your business, family members, anyone. This makes me want to re-emphasize that if you are going into business with other individuals, even family members, you should get a professional such as a lawyer or CPA to help you write up the bylaws of your company. You need a clear and understandable guide as to how the business will affect everyone involved.

That said, there are many advantages to incorporating. One advantage is the officers and stockholders are protected from the debts and liabilities of the corporation. This is because a corporation is a separate legal entity. It has its own life. It can be bought and sold or passed on to future generations. It could conceivably go on forever. Another advantage is capital can be raised through the sale of stock. Many small corporations have become huge this way.

One big disadvantage to a smaller corporation is that unless an S Corp status is applied for incorporating opens the door to double taxation on the profits of your company. This means the corporation is taxed on its profits as income and also the shareholders are taxed on the profits of the corporation as income to the shareholders. If the corporation plans to remain rather small, an election to become an S Corp would be desirable and the double taxation would be avoided. An S Corp does not get its profits taxed as income. The profits or losses are passed straight through to the shareholders. So the shareholders report the income or loss which is generated by the S Corp on their individual tax returns. This is proportionate to the percentages held by each officer/shareholder of the corporation. So, if you are just one person, like I am in my little S Corp, you are President, Vice President, Secretary, Treasurer and Number One Employee and Stockholder! This also means I am 100% responsible for the profit or loss of my business at tax time.

There are just a few rules to maintain S Corp status. First in order to be considered an S Corp you have to apply for this status with the IRS. Apply for S Corp status after you have completed all the other steps for incorporation as directed by the state you are incorporating in. This is done by filling out the IRS Form 2553. You cannot, as of this writing, fill this out and submit it online. You have to download it, print it out, fill it in and mail it to them. I suggest mailing it by certified mail so you have confirmation of the date someone at their end received it. In order to be considered an S Corp for the current year, you would have had to have sent in this form either last year sometime or no later than March 15th of this year. You can send it in any time after March 15th to be considered an S Corp for the following year.

A few more S Corp stipulations are the corporation must be a domestic corporation, you can only have one class of stock, you cannot have more than 35 stockholders, and the stockholders must be individuals or estates or certain trusts. And even if your S Corp is just you, you must pay yourself a "reasonable wage". So you do become an employee of your corporation. You have at least social security and medicare taken out of your check. Currently the rate for both is 7.65%. The corporation does match that percentage when it pays the payroll taxes to the IRS for the payroll. The bonus is you, as the officer of the corporation can also take a "dividend distribution". This has no payroll taxes taken from it. It is essentially a draw, as in a sole proprietorship. It does not affect the bottom line net profits of your corporation. And you as an individual are mostly not taxed on it at income tax time. There are formulas to help your tax professional decide which portion of your dividend distributions are taxable. You may be responsible for paying a periodic estimated tax on these distributions. For this current information you should definitely contact your CPA.

LLC = Limited Liability Company

So, contrary to popular belief, the initials LLC do not mean Limited Liability Corporation. There is no such legal term. They actually do mean Limited Liability Company. This business structure has very similar characteristics to an S Corp. So if you read the previous paragraphs on Incorporation and S Corp, you can get an idea of the LLC structure. The LLC has the limited liability advantages of a corporation. The owners are called Members and the Members are protected from the debts and liabilities of the company. Just like in an S Corp, you can be a "Single Member". So you can be an LLC all on your own. The LLC enjoys the same freedom from double taxation as the S Corp does. Meaning each Member is responsible for reporting their share of the profit or loss of the company on their individual income tax returns. A difference from the S Corp is the LLC Member is not required to receive a "reasonable wage" and does not have to be considered an employee. But an LLC Member is considered to be self-employed and is responsible for paying their own estimated taxes and self-employment tax on the income they do receive from the LLC, however the Member receives it.

Forming an LLC is very similar to forming a corporation. Start your LLC and follow the same guidelines as mentioned in the paragraphs for the description of Incorporation. An LLC has a written operating agreement or articles of organization. This is the document that will specify the time or qualifying event for dissolution of the LLC. This is another difference from a corporation. An LLC has a set length decided upon by the organizing Members. When an LLC liquidates articles of dissolution must be filed with the Secretary of State in which the LLC was formed.

Nonprofit Corporation

A Nonprofit Corporation is established for a religious, charitable, educational, artistic, literary or scientific purpose permitted under 501(c)(3) of the tax code. Qualifying Nonprofits are granted tax-exempt status by both federal and state authorities.

Articles of Incorporation must be filed with the proper state agency. In Washington it is the Secretary of State. This document must contain specific paragraphs describing the exact nature of the nonprofit activities. The nonprofit also must include the adoption of a set of Bylaws as part of its formalities. You must apply for tax exempt status from the state in which you are incorporated as well as the federal government.

For the Nonprofit Corporation to qualify for the 501(c)(3) federal tax exempt status, the IRS Form 1023 must be filled out and submitted within 15 months after the Nonprofit has been officially organized. The federal tax exemption status is effective retroactively to the date the Articles of Incorporation were filed. Once approved: the company is exempt from payment of federal corporate income taxes; it may receive both public and private grants; and all donations and contributions made to the Nonprofit can be assured to be tax deductible of up to 50% of the donor's income.

Some states require the Nonprofit to have a minimum of 3 directors, some only one and some can have less than 3 if the Nonprofit has less than 3 members. You should check with your Secretary of State's office to find out what the requirements in your state are. As of this writing, in Washington, only one is necessary. The Nonprofit can have paid employees who have regular payroll taxes taken out of their checks. Then the Nonprofit is responsible for filing the usual periodic payroll taxes that go along with creating paychecks.

Nonprofit Corporations also enjoy the same limited liability protection as profit corporations. Meaning the directors, trustees, officers and/or members are typically not personally liable for the debts and obligations of the Nonprofit. Another similarity the Nonprofit shares with the profit corporation is its unlimited life. Once a Nonprofit Corporation is created, like any other corporation, it is its own legal entity that can go on forever.

As always, if there is anything you are uncertain about and feel you do need to have a professional help you with any of the procedures necessary to get your business structured in the way that is most advantageous for you by all means do contact your Lawyer or CPA for questions or help. A little money spent on doing things correctly in the beginning will be good insurance for the duration of your business.

Why Do I Need to Have a Bookkeeping System?

Business owners who have tried really hard but have found the whole bookkeeping thing to be totally overwhelming ask this question out of frustration. If you can relate to this sentiment in any way, I want you to know you have my empathy, you really do. The point is that if you are established in a business you need a bookkeeping system. Some business's bookkeeping systems consist solely of a shoebox stuffed full of receipts. This is one way to do it, but not the most effective way. For one thing, this way will cost you a lot when you hand your shoebox to your very-expensive-per-hour accountant at tax time and pay that person to sort it out for you, when you could have done it yourself throughout the year. A good bookkeeping system is easy to maintain daily, weekly, or monthly, depending on your volume of transactions.

Use your bookkeeping system to keep track of your cash flow: Your money coming in and your money going out. You can break down your expenses so you can see how much is going to what areas of your business each month. Likewise, you can break down your income so you can see what areas are most profitable. Keep track of your equipment and major purchases you have made to run your business. A bookkeeping system will allow you to stay on top of your bank accounts and investments. Keep track of your draws. Provide you with a system to bill your customers and keep track of who owes you. Very handy! Create a system for paying bills and keep track of whom you owe so you can make payments on time and save yourself that extra finance charge. That way you won't end up paying for things twice. Do your own taxes, payroll, state and otherwise. The list is endless and all good reasons for having a well-maintained bookkeeping system. You really can do all these things.

This may sound like a long list of things to do. But, if you do it periodically, in small amounts, instead of once a year, it is easy and manageable. The rest of this book will break down all the how's and why's of how to get yourself up and running in an easy to manage bookkeeping system of your own. If you are using an easy accounting software program on your computer, this book will help you understand why things get entered the way they do. If you are going to be keeping your bookkeeping system manually, let me suggest you get a few columnar books. Get a couple that have 3 columns (one you can mark "plus", one for "minus", and one for "balance"). On each page you can set up one of your general ledger accounts and keep track of each transaction you make. As you read the following chapters you will see how this will be helpful, and you can set it all up in one big notebook. Or have a couple notebooks, one as a "sales or income journal", one as an "expense journal". You can keep it as simple as you want. These activities will help you keep up the habit of entering your transactions that I am about to describe on the upcoming pages. You may also want to get one of the larger 13 column books so you can create a spreadsheet on various sections, such as your total income or expenses, compare them with the months before, and so forth. As you read on I hope to help you develop some good methods and practices. Just remember keep it simple!

First Part: Set Up Your "Chart of Accounts"
and Filing System

What is a "Chart of Accounts"? This is your list of "General Ledger Accounts". This is the map of everything financial in your company.

In your Chart of Accounts you have several sections. I will briefly explain them as we go along. Later I will explain how they fit together, how you make entries to them, and why you need them set up this way. So here they are, in order:

1) **Assets:** This is where you set up anything that will be an asset to your company for a period of time (like months or years). "Current" Assets are accounts such as Bank Accounts, your Accounts Receivable (those are the accounts of your customers that owe you money on time, not cash sales), or Inventory, to name a few. "Fixed" Assets are, for example, the values of Major Equipment Purchases ("Fixed" Assets means they aren't going anywhere unless you get rid of them some how), the "Fair Market Value" of Land or Property owned by your business (another "Fixed" asset). Anything that continually adds to the worth of your company.

2) **Liabilities:** These are the debts your company accumulates to be paid at a later date or to be continually paid on for long periods of time. If there is a Loan to your company, the rule of thumb for judging a "Long Term" Liability versus a "Current" Liability is this: if the loan period is a year or longer, it is a Long Term Liability. Anything owed which will take less than a year to pay is a Current Liability. Some examples of Liability Accounts are: Accounts such as Loans made to your company (car loans, equipment loans, property loans), Accounts Payable (those are the accounts of your vendors that you owe money to on time, not cash purchases), any Taxes Payable accounts (payroll taxes, your state's sales tax, or federal taxes that are accumulated as you conduct business and are paid periodically).

3) **Equity:** This is where you keep track of what you personally put into and take out of the company. These are your Draw Accounts (money you remove from the company for personal use), Owner Investment Account (money you have taken from your personal resources and injected into your business). This is also the area where you list your company's Retained Earnings and Net Income Accounts. Your Net Income shows your company's "Net Profits" for a given time period and is accumulated throughout your company's fiscal year. This account will start over again from zero with the new fiscal year. The Retained Earnings Account is where your cumulative Net Profit is reflected, ("Retained"), on a permanent basis. This account does not zero out at any time. It continues to reflect the fiscal year changes in your Net Profits from year to year.

13

4) **Income:** Just what it says. This is the income you receive from your customers whether you have sent them a bill or made a cash sale. This is where it gets recorded. More on how that works later on. This is also a place to list "Reimbursed Expenses", which act as offsetting accounts to certain expenses, such as Shipping or Travel Expenses.

5) **Cost of Goods Sold:** These are your first Expense Accounts. These accounts are where you record purchases you make for the sole purpose of operating your business. Things like Merchandise for Inventory if you're in retail, or Parts that go into the machines you make, or Food, Beer and Wine for your restaurant, or Gravel and Asphalt for the roads you pave, you get the idea. Some people also like to include in this section Wages Paid, or Shipping Costs.

6) **General and Administrative Expenses:** These are your next set of Expense Accounts. These accounts are your Bank Charges, Consultation Fees, Donations, Equipment Rental, Finance Charges, Maintenance and Repair, Utilities, Entertainment and Travel, Licenses, Permits, Professional Services (lawyers and accountants), Wages, and any expensed Taxes like Payroll, State or Federal Taxes, Auto Expenses, Insurance, on and on. If you are just starting out and you want to keep it simple, here is a good rule of thumb: get a copy of the IRS tax form **Schedule C** for a Form 1040. You can download it from http://www.irs.ustreas.gov/formspubs/index.html Use this as a guideline for setting up your General Expense accounts. It has every expense that the IRS allows for a small business (in particular a sole proprietorship), to report at tax time. These are the ones that count. You may find that you want to make your expense accounts more detailed so they make more sense to your particular situation. You can do this as the need arises; you can break down your expense accounts at any time as you go along. But the Schedule C is a good starting guide.

7) **Other Income and Expenses:** Finally! Last section. This has two areas in one. Other Income is Interest Income, or Uncategorized or Miscellaneous Income accounts, the nebulous stuff can be held here until you find a better place for it. It actually is better if you can stay away from using the Uncategorized or Miscellaneous accounts if possible; it will be one less explanation you have to make should anyone of importance come to scrutinize your "details". That's why I say just use it until you find a better place to put it. I check my Miscellaneous Accounts once a month. They are like little flags that let me know there is something I need to deal with before I close off the month's business. Other Expenses are a little different from Other Income. Other Expenses is where to put things like Depreciation Expense and Amortization Expense (I will explain how you incur these expenses later on). Generally these are expense accounts that don't have a direct affect on the running of your business, but are still a part of your monthly financial picture. There are also Uncategorized or Miscellaneous Expense accounts, just like the Other Income accounts, and the same suggestion for use of these accounts applies in this area as well.

Here is an example of a Chart of Accounts for a typical retail business as a sole proprietorship.

- **Note:** These following examples will all be based on the sole proprietorship style of business setup, as it is the easiest as far as filing taxes at the end of the year and a good way to start out if you are new and want a simple setup. However, based on your unique specifics such as how large your company will be, your volume of expected income, or how many people involved in running it, etc. you may want to consider other set ups such as an S Corporation or an LLC, for example. You should thoroughly explore the tax and legal benefits of other types of business setups. If you are interested in other forms of business you should definitely consult the advice of your CPA or Lawyer. Also, please note however, that for our purposes here in this book, the basic bookkeeping setup explained on the following pages is going to be the same no matter what style of business you choose to set up. The only difference is corporations and LLCs may have a few additional general ledger accounts not mentioned here. But bookkeeping and accounting basics are all the same for any business!

Chart of Accounts

Business Checking	Asset
Business Savings	Asset
Accounts Receivable	Asset
Inventory	Asset
Major Equipment	Asset (Fixed)
Equipment Depreciation	Asset (Fixed)
Accounts Payable	Liability (Current)
Payroll Tax Payable	Liability (Current)
State Sales Tax Payable	Liability (Current)
Federal Tax Payable	Liability (Current)
Bank Note Payable	Liability (Long Term or Current)
Auto Loan Payable	Liability (Long Term or Current)
Owner Draws	Equity
Owner Investment	Equity
Net Income	Equity
Retained Earnings	Equity

Resale Income	Income
Wholesale Income	Income
Discounts and Returns	Income
Reimbursed Expenses	Income
Resale Merchandise	Cost of Goods Sold
Advertising	Expense
Automobile Expenses	Expense
Bank Charges	Expense
Contributions	Expense
Dues and Subscriptions	Expense
Equipment Rental	Expense
Insurance	Expense
Interest Expense	Expense
Licenses and Permits	Expense
Payroll Wages	Expense
Payroll Taxes	Expense
Postage and Delivery	Expense
Professional Fees	Expense
Rent	Expense
Repairs and Maintenance	Expense
Supplies	Expense
Taxes-State & Federal	Expense
Travel and Entertainment	Expense
Utilities	Expense
Interest Income	Other Income
Miscellaneous Income	Other Income
Depreciation Expense	Other Expense
Miscellaneous Expense	Other Expense

This is just a basic start-up listing of a Chart of Accounts. As you record financial entries for your business, each of these accounts will provide homes for all of those entries. As I mentioned earlier, when you get along in your business you may find a need for more detailed accounts or even "Sub-Accounts" (e.g. Auto Expense can have Sub-Accounts for Fuel and Repairs, or Utilities can have Sub-Accounts of Telephone and Electricity), so that your list of General Ledger Accounts makes more sense to <u>you</u>.

Once you figure out what accounts you want to start your Chart of Accounts with you will want to create a file system to keep all the paper in. To start with, these will be receipts, bank statements, all utility bills, any tax forms such as payroll or sales tax, and invoices from purchases you have made for your business. For a simple start up filing system I find it easiest to just get a box of large manila envelopes. I keep the receipts, bank statements, invoices and tax forms for each month in one of the envelopes. I mark the outside of the envelope "JULY 2008" for example. And then just simply put all the paper for that month into that envelope and put it in a storage box that will contain the year "2008".

Or, if you know your business is going to be larger and a little more complicated than that, get a file cabinet. Keep your paper in alphabetical order in file folders in the file drawers and then clean it out into a well-marked box once a year.

Once you get a handle on your filing system, here is how long you must keep all the important papers you will be accumulating:

Keep for 3 Years:

Bank statements

Deposit slips

Insurance policies

General correspondence

Keep for 4 years:

Invoices to customers

Cash expenditure receipts

Expense reports by/for employees

Keep for 7 years:

Accounts payable documents

Accounts receivable documents

Cancelled checks

Notes receivable paperwork (paid off)

Payroll records

Employee/personnel records

Inventory records and invoices

Keep Permanently:

Chart of accounts/General ledgers

Legal correspondence

Mortgage paperwork

Financial statements

Notes payable paperwork

Property appraisals and records

Tax returns and related documents

Trademark registrations

I know what you are thinking! Yes it does pile up! And fast too! I know some small businesses that are so big and old they have to actually rent a storage space just to keep all their old paper in. But make no mistake here; it is worth it most definitely! If you ever get audited for <u>anything</u> by <u>any</u> government echelon there is absolutely no greater satisfaction than to be able to quickly and easily put your hands on the pile of paper they want to examine!

Or think of this situation: What if you have to prove you've paid for something and when you paid it? Or what if you have to prove to someone else <u>they</u> never paid <u>you</u> and when you billed them?

So make certain you create a good filing system from the beginning and keep all the old paper for the recommended amounts of time. Eventually you will be very glad you did!

Entering Your Information
(The Core of Accounting Principles)

What I am about to explain here is really the core of accounting principles. Once you get this mode of thinking down, you will have everything down. Seriously. Clear your mind, right now, of the way your bank talks to you, and of balance sheets or any other financial statements. Just focus on this and very soon you will see how it all fits together.

In bookkeeping you always make entries called "Double Sided Entries". That means for every one entry made there has to be a counter entry made. These are called "Debits and Credits". Regarding your General Ledger Accounts, a Debit can be a plus OR a minus, and a Credit can be a plus OR a minus. This all depends on what account you are dealing with. Are you with me so far? OK, that's one thing to remember.

Depending on how an amount gets ADDED to an account determines if that account is called a Debit Account or a Credit Account. So, remember the Chart of Accounts from the previous pages? This is how these accounts are classified according to Debits and Credits:

Asset = Debit

Liability = Credit

Equity = Credit

Income = Credit

Cost of Goods Sold = Debit

Expense = Debit

Other Income = Credit

Other Expense = Debit

When REMOVING amounts from your general ledger accounts the amount removed is the opposite from the debit or credit, whichever is appropriate. (Examples are coming up!) So our list of general ledger accounts for the sake of double-sided entries will function this way:

Asset Accounts:	Debit = (+)	Credit = (-)
Liability Accounts:	Debit = (-)	Credit = (+)
Equity Accounts:	Debit = (-)	Credit = (+)
Income Accounts:	Debit = (-)	Credit = (+)
Cost of Goods Sold:	Debit = (+)	Credit = (-)
Expense Accounts:	Debit = (+)	Credit = (-)
Other Income Accounts:	Debit = (-)	Credit = (+)
Other Expense Accounts:	Debit = (+)	Credit = (-)

When you make your entries, remember, all your entries have to have counter entries. This is how we keep the "books in balance". An easy way to start out on this new way of thinking is to imagine a **"T".** As you are figuring out what goes where it helps to take a piece of paper and draw this T. On the LEFT side of the T write "Debit" (can be abbreviated DR, don't ask me why), and on the RIGHT side of the T write "Credit" (can be abbreviated using CR), like this: DR | CR

These are called "T Accounts" (appropriate!) **Note:** Debit is always on the left and Credit is always on the right regardless if either is a plus or a minus.

   OK, I know you are dying to see this in action, so let's do a simple entry using the "T Accounts". Say you need some paper and an ink cartridge for your printer, and you also noticed your supply of pens have somehow all walked out the door. So you go to your neighborhood office supply store with your company check book, write out a check for these items, and take them back to your office. Now you need to log your purchase. If you have a neat accounting program on your computer, you just call up your check register, enter the date, check number, who the check was written to, the amount, designate "Office Supplies" for your account, and in "Memo" write "Pens, Paper and Ink", hit enter and you're done! But what your accounting software is actually doing for you is based on our "T Accounts". The entry the software made looks like this:

Checking	Office Supplies
DR	CR	DR	CR
$25.00	$25.00

So what actually took place was this: Cash was REMOVED from the Checking Account, which is an Asset Account, which means it is a Debit Account, so when we remove an amount from that account it is a CREDIT entry. The other thing that took place was we ADDED to the Office Supplies, which is an Expense Account, which means it also is a Debit Account, so when we add to that account it is a DEBIT entry. See how the T Accounts can graphically help you see what is actually going to where? No??

   Let's do another simple entry. Let's say someone comes into your place and wants to purchase some merchandise. They are going to pay for it on the spot so it is a cash sale. You are a retailer, therefore, if you are in most states, you must also charge sales tax which you accumulate and pay all at once to the state at a later time. Here's how this entry looks in
T Accounts:

Checking	Sales	Sales Tax Payable
DR	CR	DR	CR	DR	CR
$52.50	$50.00	$2.50

See how we used two credit entries to balance the one debit entry? This is why: We ADDED to the Checking Account, which is an Asset Account and therefore a Debit Account. So when we add to that account it is a DEBIT entry. We also ADDED to the Sales Account, which is an Income Account and therefore a Credit Account. So when we add to that account it is a CREDT entry. Lastly, we also ADDED to the Sales Tax Payable Account, which is a Liability Account (because we are accumulating it to be paid at a later date). So when we add to that account it is also a CREDIT entry. By the way, if you live in a state with Sales Tax a helpful resource is your state's tax agency's website. In Washington it is http://dor.wa.gov

I'll show you a couple more appropriate entries. Say you have a really good, regular customer. They buy retail (as opposed to wholesale), so you have to charge sales tax, if you are in most states. They call up and want you to send them some merchandise in the mail and they will pay you thirty days later, so they want you to bill them for the product. This one transaction would have two series of entries to follow through with. Here's how it looks in T Accounts:

Entry #1:   Retail Sales   Sales Tax Payable   Shipping (Reimbursed Expense)

DR	CR	DR	CR	DR	CR
$50.00	$2.50	$2.50

Accounts Receivable ("Mr. Really Good Customer")

DR	CR
$55.00

The balance of Mr. Really Good Customer's account is now being stored in your Accounts Receivable Account. Which is an Asset account, therefore a Debit account and we ADDED to it so this one Debit entry was balanced out using three Credit entries. Did you follow along? Here is the flip side to this:

Entry #2: (Mr. Really Good Customer pays thirty days later):

Checking	Accounts Receivable
DR	CR	DR	CR
$55.00	$55.00

Now that the customer paid, you will ADD his payment to the Checking Account and REMOVE the balance that he owes you from your Accounts Receivable Account. See the "ins" and "outs" of this? Why is it logged this way? Because you always want to record a transaction on the day the transaction was completed. Recording transactions out of period is the cause of many headaches and a great deal of puzzlement in bookkeeping! Let's say that when Mr. Really Good Customer called it was September 20th. Maybe it took you two days to get everything together for his order and you shipped it on September 23rd. Now September 23rd is the date on his invoice that you sent to him with his order. But Mr. Really Good Customer won't be sending you a check until October 20th. Even though your checking account will not reflect his payment until October, you still need to show that the sale was made in September. This is for the sake of budgeting, forecasting, and comparison. That is why there is an Accounts Receivable account to store customer balances until they pay. And that is why there needs to be two series of entries for this one transaction.

- **Note:** This is called "**Accrual** Based" accounting, (as opposed to "**Cash** Based" accounting). In Cash Based accounting there is no need for this because everything is recorded as sold or paid for as the end of the transaction takes place. You only record the transaction as you write the check for the expense or receive the money for the bill owed to you. Because of this, Cash Based accounting is a little easier. In the Cash Based accounting method debits and credits and all the principles we have discussed so far still apply. But I personally like Accrual Based accounting as a more effective way of avoiding problems in cash flow, budgeting and so forth. This is because we are recording the transactions on the date they occur and storing them in our assets or liabilities until they are to be paid on or received. This way we can plan ahead and make well educated business decisions, and manage cash flow much better. So in these past explanations and those to follow, keep in mind I am basing my methods on Accrual Based accounting. Of course you may choose to set up your small business based on either method. You should make a decision on one method or the other to keep your bookkeeping system consistent. Also when tax time comes around your accountant should ask you if you are operating on an Accrual or Cash Based accounting system. Once you start filing a certain way with your state government or the IRS, you shouldn't change it from year to year.

It works exactly the same way with your Accounts Payable Account. Think in reverse. You receive a bill for some merchandise you ordered, and you are the Really Good Customer. But you are buying wholesale because you are intending to re-sell it to your customer and you will put the sales tax on it at that point. (If you are in a state where sales tax is charged, you will not be paying tax on this merchandise at your point of purchase, but your customer will pay sales tax when he buys it from you.) So they give you thirty days to pay. Well, for all the same reasons, you want to record that expense according to the date on the invoice that your vendor sent to you. Your transaction for this is also two series of entries. It looks like this:

Entry #1: Resale Merchandise (Cost of Goods Sold)   Shipping (Expense Account)

DR	CR
$50.00	

DR	CR
$2.50	

Accounts Payable (Acme Merchandise)

DR	CR
	$52.50

Your Accounts Payable account is a Liability account, therefore a Credit account. So when we ADD to Accounts Payable it is a Credit entry. See how it took the two Debit entries to balance the one Credit entry? Now you are holding your balance due to Acme Merchandise in your Accounts Payable account until you get ready to pay it thirty days later. You want to record your expense in the month in which it was incurred. So, now it's thirty days later, you're paying your bills, here is the flip side to this transaction:

Entry #2:

Checking   Accounts Payable

DR	CR
	$52.50

DR	CR
$52.50	

See how this is working together? OK, one more transaction. This one is a bit complex. If you can follow along on this one, you don't need to read this chapter over again! Say you want to buy a machine for your shop. It will cost $10,000.00! You don't happen to have the cash available so you go to the bank. They say OK; they give you five years to pay it off at 5% interest. (Nice Bank!). This will take one major transaction and five years worth of monthly transactions to accomplish. But once you set it up, no problem. Here's how this looks in T Accounts:

Main Entry:

Capitalized Equipment   Note Payable (Nice Bank)

DR	CR
$10,000.00	

DR	CR
	$10,000.00

Well, that part was easy. The Capitalized Equipment is a Fixed Asset Account. This is where you will hold the full value of your equipment, to be depreciated monthly over the next five years. (We will discuss Depreciation in greater detail later on.) This is good because beefing up your assets makes your company look pretty good on paper to the people who care about things like that. The Note Payable to the Nice Bank is now a Long Term Liability Account, because it will take you five years to pay it. So, here

23

are the entries you will be making on a monthly basis to reduce the note, record the interest expense and depreciate the equipment:

#1: Note Reduction:

Checking		Note Payable-Nice Bank		Interest Expense	
DR	CR	DR	CR	DR	CR
	$189.00	$147.00		$42.00	

#2: Depreciation Expense:

Accumulated Depreciation		Depreciation Expense	
DR	CR	DR	CR
	$167.00	$167.00	

OK, what did we do?? Well, time came to make your first payment. Using your handy loan calculation program on your computer, OR getting the loan payment amortization schedule from your Nice Bank, you saw your monthly payment was to be $189.00 per month. Out of this a portion goes to the principle on the note and the rest is interest expense. Take advantage of interest expense as a write off against profits, while the principle portion of your payment reduces your Liabilities by reducing your Note Payable. The loan payment amortization schedule is a handy thing to have because it shows exactly what the portions are each month so you can keep in step with the bank. If you don't have one for your loans, get one! Next you might have called your CPA to find out about depreciation. You can do this yourself on a monthly basis. The rule of thumb is to take the value of the equipment and divide it, for example, by 60 months, which is 5 years. This is called the "Straight Line Depreciation Method" and is based on the assumption that the average life of your asset is five years. Time periods may vary depending on the type of asset it is (land, computers, heavy equipment, signage, etc..), if you are unsure, this is a question worthy of your CPA's time. Otherwise, it is a very simple way to capture your depreciation expense on a monthly basis. Your CPA may make an adjustment to this at the end of the year. The Accumulated Depreciation Account is a "Negative Asset" account. It immediately follows the Capitalized Equipment Account. It is an Asset Account, but you add to it by making a Credit entry, it will appear as having a negative balance on your financial reports. This is correct and as it should be. You are slowly reducing the value of your fixed assets with depreciation. Taking depreciation on your capital assets can save you a lot in taxes. It is a good way to add to your expenses to reduce your profits without affecting your cash flow.

There, was that painless? This is the way things get entered into your General Ledger Accounts. So if you are working late one night and catching up all the transactions of your business day, you will know you did everything 100% correctly IF at the end of all your entries, your Debits EQUAL your Credits. By now I'm sure you see how this is one of your main goals in entering your information. If you are doing this all manually, (without the aid of a nifty, easy to use accounting software program on your computer), you should definitely take the time to add up both sides of your columns. If for some reason your Debits do not equal your Credits, you must find out where you are "out of balance" and make the necessary correction. Because if you don't, you may be chasing a bookkeeping "ghost" for a while and that is a headache!   If you are using a handy accounting software program, it probably will not let you record the transaction if you are out of balance in any way. That's just the way they are, and that is a good thing!

The Basic Financial Reports

There are many financial reports that you can make for your company based on all your entries collectively. You can get as detailed and as complex as you want. You can make as many reports as you want to suit your needs. You can make reports for budgeting, forecasting or planning. You can make them just on your sales or just on your expenses. If you use a spreadsheet program, you can really go to town!

But, for the sake of simplicity, (our main goal here), I will just discuss the three basic financial reports that are necessary to every business. They are the Trial Balance, the Profit and Loss or Income Statement, and the Balance Sheet. You should try to do these monthly or at least quarterly, (every 3 months). Don't wait to do them every six months or yearly. If there are any errors to be corrected, it is much easier to remember back a couple weeks ago than eight months ago! Besides that, as you see how useful this information is, you will want to do them on a very regular basis to aid yourself in budgeting, forecasting, and planning.

#1 The Trial Balance

This is, (as you may suspect from the name), a try-out report to make sure all your Debits equal your Credits. The entire Chart of Accounts, that is all your general ledger accounts, are listed. Their current balances, as of whatever day you choose, are listed in either the Debit column or Credit column, depending on if they are Debit Accounts or Credit Accounts. This is just one long list without discernment to whether they are assets, liabilities, expenses, etc.. Here is an example of a Trial Balance with a very simple Chart of Accounts, for the months of January thru September:

Trial Balance Jan. 1st - Sept. 30th	Debit	Credit
Cash in Bank	7,000.00	
Accounts Receivable	599.00	
Capitalized Equipment	3,200.00	
Accumulated Depreciation		799.97
Federal Taxes Payable		99.00
Owner Investments		3,200.00
Owner Draws	567.96	
Retained Earnings	255.00	
Consulting Income		10,725.00
Other Regular Income		358.50
Advertising	5.00	
Office Supplies	281.94	
Postage and Delivery	84.42	
Rent	40.00	
Taxes	1,749.00	
Telephone	23.41	
Business Meals	166.72	
Business Travel	730.05	
Depreciation Expense	479.97	
Totals:	**15,182.47**	**15,182.47**

- **Note:** When you are making any kind of a financial report, it is customary to always draw a double bottom line at the end of your bottom lines

See how that is? This is a great Trial Balance because all the balances in the Debit column add up to the same amount as all the balances in the Credit column. If you try making your Trial Balance and the debits do not equal the credits, guess what? You have to go back and find out where you have made your mistake. If you are doing this manually, it could take some work. But it really is worth it to find the trouble. You can start by making certain you have made all your entries through the date you have chosen for your report. For instance, are all your Accounts Receivable Invoices entered? Are all the payments you have received from your customers entered? Have you entered all the checks you have written through this date and are they entered to the correct accounts? Did you enter a Debit amount as a Credit amount (or vice versa)? Have you reconciled your checking account to your bank statement, etc.. (This is another great reason to have a simple accounting software program; problems of this nature will be very rare!) So when your Trial Balance is in check, you can move on to the next reports.

- **A Bookkeeping Trick:** Take the amount your debits and credits are off. If this amount can be divided by two this is a good indication the problem could be an amount incorrectly entered as a debit or a credit when it should be the other way around. Try this test first, it may make problem solving easier. This same test also applies to balancing your bank accounts to their statements. A check could have been entered as a deposit, or vice versa.

#2 The Profit and Loss (or Income) Statement

To make it simple, I just call this report the "P & L". Now is the time to start segregating the General Ledger accounts into their respective classifications. This is a report on the Income, Cost of Goods Sold, Expense, Other Income and Other Expense accounts from the General Ledger Chart of Accounts. Here is an example of a "P & L" using the information from the Trial Balance listed previously:

Profit & Loss Statement Jan. 1st – Sept. 30th

Income

Consulting Income	10,725.00
Other Regular Income	358.50
Total Income	**11,083.50**

Expense

Advertising	5.00
Office Supplies	281.94
Postage and Delivery	84.42
Rent	40.00
Taxes (Federal)	1,749.00
Telephone	23.41
Meals	166.72
Travel	730.05
Total Expense	**3,080.54**

Other Expense

Depreciation	479.97
Total Other Expense	**479.97**
Net Income	**7,522.99**

See how I got the Net Income figure? This is an important figure because it will be carried onto the next (and final) report, which is the Balance Sheet, coming up. But first, please note this P & L does not have a Cost of Goods Sold section, because it is not a retail or manufacturing company, this is a service company. So therefore it has no Cost of Goods Sold accounts. If you have Cost of Goods Sold accounts to add to your report, they will fit in between the Income and the Expense account sections and will be subtracted from the Income total like the other Expense sections.

Now, all Income, Cost of Goods Sold, and Expense accounts have one thing in common, and that is at the end of the company's fiscal year, all these totals get "zeroed out". If you are on an easy to use accounting software program, this will take place automatically. If you are doing this manually, these entries will have to be made. Your income accounts will all have Debit entries to zero them out. Your cost of goods sold and expense accounts will all have Credit entries to zero them out. Your balancing entry against all these will be to your Retained Earnings account; this is the total of all the entries of both the Debits and Credits. This is explained in more detail in the next report, the "Balance Sheet".

Once again, please note that this report is for the time period Jan. 1st through Sept. 30th and the account totals are the year to date totals for that period. You can do a P & L report any time. You can do it for a day, a week, a month, a year. You can create percentages of your expense accounts against your income. For instance, in the example above, the total expense for Federal Taxes so far through this point in this company's fiscal year is 15.78% (!) of the total income figure. You can also use percentages of expense and income to plan your purchasing better. How much you are making compared to how much you are spending in a certain area or department? You can do comparison P & L's. You can have two columns on your report one with a heading of August Current Year the other with August Previous Year and list the accounts as usual with each of those month's totals. You can use this report for budgeting and forecasting. Make a simulated P & L for next year and see how you do when you make your actual P & L. See the eleven billion uses for this report?? Let's see how it fits together with the next report.

#3 The Balance Sheet

The Balance Sheet is a report on Assets, Liabilities and Equity. One reason this is called the Balance Sheet is because the total amount of your Assets must equal the sum of your Liabilities + Equity.

Assets = Liabilities + Equity

If that takes place, then you know you have done a good job in putting together your Balance Sheet. Here is an example of a Balance Sheet using the information from the Trial Balance listed previously:

Balance Sheet Jan. 1st - Sept. 30th

Assets

Cash in Bank	7,000.00
Accounts Receivable	599.00
Capitalized Equipment	3,200.00
Accumulated Depreciation	-799.97
Total Assets	**9,999.03**

Liabilities

Federal Tax Payable	99.00

Equity

Owner Investment	3,200.00
Owner Draws	-567.96
Retained Earnings	-255.00
Net Income	7,522.99
Total Liabilities & Equity	**9,999.03**

This is a great Balance Sheet because the total of all the Asset balances is the same as when the Liabilities are added to the Equity Accounts.

Now that you have an example in front of you, let's talk a little about the Balance Sheet. This is a report on all your accounts that have continuous balances. The general ledger accounts reported on here do NOT get "zeroed out" at the end of the fiscal year and started over. They are ongoing, reflecting the changes accordingly as you add to them or take from them for the duration of the company. There are only two exceptions in these accounts. They are the Owner Draw account and Net Income. At the beginning of every fiscal year, the balances in these two accounts are zero. This is true for the draw account because imagine if you kept accumulating all your draws for 5 years! It would throw your company's equity picture all out of proportion. And, this is true for the Net Income because this number is a carryover from our previous report, the Profit and Loss or Income Statement. The accounts reported on the P & L Statement all get zeroed out for the start of the new fiscal year, no exceptions. So that makes our Net Income figure start over as well. The Net Income is the "year to date" balance after you subtract all your expense accounts from all your income accounts. The figure that appears on your Balance Sheet is for your fiscal year up through the date you are reporting on. For instance, this Balance Sheet is for January through September. Therefore, this Net Income figure is the year to date net profit for nine months worth of income less nine months worth of expenses. It appears on the Balance Sheet for a couple of reasons. For one thing it is very much a part of your company's equity picture. The other thing is, because the Balance Sheet is a report on the cumulative accounts for your company, Net Income fits that criteria as well.

The other equity account, Retained Earnings, is like the "dump" account for zeroing out these items on the first day of the new fiscal year. Retained Earnings are Profits (or Losses) from earlier Accounting Periods that are cumulative and remaining "in the company", they are not being distributed back to the company's owner(s). At the end of your fiscal year your Owner Draw Account is transferred into Retained Earnings. Then the Retained Earnings balance remains the same throughout the year, always reflecting the cumulative total of your previous year's Net Profits. Here's an example:

Say I've already zeroed out my Income and Expense accounts, (as mentioned previously in the "Profit and Loss" explanation), and dumped the resulting balance of that into my Retained Earnings account. Now I want to zero out my draw account for my company because I am about to start my new fiscal year, it is my first day. And I have drawn a total of $10,000.00 from my company throughout the previous year. Remember Equity Accounts are Credit Accounts. My draw account is a Debit balance or negative balance (because I have been "taking from" my company). So I need to ADD to it to make it zero. So in "T Accounts" the entries look like this:

Owner Draws		Retained Earnings	
DR	CR	DR	CR
	$10,000.00	$10,000.00	

Since my Draw account had a negative Debit balance I added the Credit amount of $10,000. This will now be removed from my Retained Earnings account which is cumulative of all my previous year's Net Profits and will appear on my Balance Sheet report as the same end result figure every time throughout the upcoming year.

Are you still with me? See how this all fits together like a bunch of puzzle pieces?? You know, if you have an easy to use accounting software program on your computer, this is all done for you automatically. If it were a truly up to date program, you wouldn't have to actually make these entries. So, now you know why your computer does what it does for you. And if you are doing your own books manually, this information is imperative to you. Grasp an understanding of these concepts described here and you can walk with total confidence into any bank, or lawyer, or CPA, or any Auditor from any agency because you will be able to believe in the integrity of your own work. Wow! That's a freedom from always having to worry about where you are at in your business, right? Let's move on to the next section.

Payroll

There are many things to know about payroll. First of all, a suggestion to you who have employees: Make sure you have them fill out a W-4 form. This is the form that has them list their name, address, social security number, and what their deduction status will be on their paycheck. You have probably filled out one of these forms before yourself. It is necessary for your quarterly and year-end reporting. And if you have had the unfortunate situation of hiring someone only to have them quit after their first paycheck, you will know how hard it may be to track them down for this information if you didn't get it from them at the very start.

So, doing your own payroll isn't hard, but payroll taxes do provide a challenge! When you do a paycheck for yourself or employees the Gross Wage, ("Gross" is the wage before any taxes are taken out), is recorded as a Debit in your expense account for "Payroll" or "Wages". Or you can define it better by calling it "Gross Wages". The payroll taxes go into the related payroll tax liability accounts as Credits. The Net amount of the paycheck, ("Net" is the wage after the taxes come out), is removed from your checkbook also as a Credit entry. Remember how the Debits and Credits are when you write a check? Let's see how this looks in "T" accounts:

(Expense)	(Current Liab.)	(Current Liab.)	(Current Liab.)
Gross Wages	Fed. Withholding	Soc.Sec. & Med.	State Disability
DR | CR	DR | CR	DR | CR	DR | CR
$500.	$65.	$38.25	$1.50

Checking
DR   \| CR
$395.25 (Net Pay Check)

See how all the credits add up to the Gross Wage Debit? It seems easy so far. The part that some people find tough about payroll is keeping track of all the taxes. Let me break them down using the above example:

A. Payroll Taxes that are the Employee's Responsibility:

#1 Federal Withholding

This also gets abbreviated as FWT or FIT (Federal Income Tax). If you are doing your payroll manually you must have an IRS publication called a "Circular E" and it must be for the current year.

Using the W-4 form that I first mentioned in this section, take note of the deduction status the employee provided (i.e. single, married, with 0, 1, or 2, etc. deductions). In the Circular E are pages of tables to help you determine the correct amount of Federal Withholding for the paycheck.

First you choose the pages that correspond to the frequency of your payroll. Do you pay employees weekly (once a week), bi-weekly (every other week), semi-monthly (twice a month), or monthly (once a month)? Then find the section that corresponds to the deduction status as listed on the employee's W-4 form. Then find the Gross Wage of the paycheck, look in the proper column, and find the correct Federal Withholding amount. Federal Withholding is paid entirely by the employee. You are merely deducting it from the paycheck for them to pass it on to the IRS for them. That is your responsibility as an employer. So, technically you are not withholding your money from the employee's check, you are withholding their money from their check for them. This is a very important point to remember as an employer. Let's look at the other taxes then I can tie these all together.

#2 Social Security and Medicare

Collectively these add up to 7.65% of the employee's Gross Wage. Separately they are: Social Security at a rate of 6.2% and this has a wage base. That means after an employee's Gross Wage reaches a certain amount in the year from January through December you don't have to withhold that out of their check any more for the remainder of that year. Currently the wage base is $84,000. Medicare is at a rate of 1.45% and this has no wage base, in other words, all wages are subject to the 1.45% Medicare. Multiply the Gross Wage by each of these percentages to get the proper deduction amount. (Note: The percentages and wage base mentioned here is current with this writing, consult your Circular E to make sure of the percentages and wage base at the time you are preparing your payroll, they do change from time to time). And again, you are simply withholding this money from your employee's check for them.

#3 Your State's Disability Insurance

This is a deduction most states have. It is based on the same premise as the federal taxes in that you withhold it from your employee's check for them. In the state of Washington this is sent to the Dept. of Labor & Industries. So, on the paycheck it is designated as Labor and Industries or just L & I. Rates of withholding vary from state to state and sometimes are contingent on the employee's job description, like it is in our state. Also, in Washington, this is not based on the employee's wage it is based on their hours. So you would multiply the employee's rate by their hours to get the proper deduction amount.

These are the usual items that are withheld from the employee's paycheck by the employer to be sent in for the employee at the appropriate time. Now we have to look at:

B. Payroll Taxes that are the Employer's Responsibility:

#1 Social Security and Medicare

This is NOT withheld from the employee's paycheck. This is an employer expense. And once again, check your Circular E publication for the current rate at the time you are reading this. Right now the employer portion of Social Security and Medicare is exactly the same rate as the employee's. And the wage base is the same too. So, when you make the payment for these items to the IRS for the employee, you make the same payment for the employer. These are totaled all together onto the same check along with the Federal Withholding amount you withheld from your employee's paycheck. The frequency of this payment depends on the size of your payroll. If the Federal Withholding, along with the Employee and Employer portions of both Social Security and Medicare are more than $500 in a quarter (Jan.-Mar., Apr.-June, July-Sept., Oct.-Dec.), then you should be making this deposit once a month on the 15th at your bank. Check with your bank to make sure they are capable of receiving payroll tax payments for the IRS. Most do, some don't. When you do pay this check at your bank it will require a "Federal Tax Deposit coupon". This is a small white and blue coupon that goes with your check stating your company name, employer ID number, and amount you are paying. You also must mark in the little oval that corresponds with the proper quarter you are paying for, and the oval marked "941". Or, if your payroll is really big, you may be required by the IRS to pay this on each payroll. If that is the case, they will let you know most likely after your first year. And now, any new companies applying for employer ID numbers are now being asked to pay these taxes electronically either by phone or via the Internet. This is easy with the instructions they send along to you. If in a quarter these combined taxes are less than $500 then you can pay it quarterly without incurring a penalty for lateness. This is done by reporting your payroll amount and total amounts of Federal Withholding, Social Security and Medicare on the IRS Form 941. It is pretty easy to fill this out yourself each quarter if you have been keeping good records of your payroll.

#2 Federal Unemployment Tax

Otherwise known as FUTA. This is a federal unemployment tax generated to cover employees who have lost their jobs. Now pretty much every employer has to pay this percentage based on their employee's Gross Wages. Again, all the really detailed information on this tax is in the Circular E. Check it for current rates and how this tax applies to your employment situation. Generally speaking, however, this tax basically mirrors your state's unemployment tax. If you are required to pay unemployment tax in your state, then you are also required to follow up with the FUTA. The current rate as of this writing for

35

FUTA is 6.2%. Most employers are eligible for a credit on this tax of 5.4%. So that leaves the total rate of FUTA at .8%. And FUTA has a wage base of, at this writing, $7,000. So that means after an employee incurs $7,000 in Gross Wages, in a year from Jan.-Dec. you don't have to pay this tax any longer for that employee for the remainder of that year. Again, this is an employer expense. This is NOT withheld from the employee's paycheck. FUTA is reported on the IRS Form 940. This form is only filed annually after December. However if your accumulated FUTA gets to be more than $100 in any quarter, you must make a check and pay it through your bank or online or over the telephone in exactly the same fashion as you pay your Federal Withholding, Social Security and Medicare. Meaning you will want to use the Federal Tax Deposit coupons with your check when you take it to your bank. Mark the proper oval for the proper quarter and mark the oval for "940". And FUTA should be paid with a separate check.

#3 State Unemployment

This is an employer expense and is NOT withheld from the employee's check. Every state is probably going to be different on this one. In our state of Washington, the rate is based on the employee's gross wage and has a pretty low wage base. But the percentage rate varies from employer to employer. They base their rates on how many claims you get against your unemployment account. This is paid on a quarterly basis using a form that gets filled out to report your total payroll, less any payroll amounts that are exempt due to the wage base, then multiplying what is left by the employer's rate and that's what is owed for that quarter. Please check with your state's department for unemployment for information on how you are to report for your payroll.

#4 Your State's Disability Insurance

Some states, for instance our state of Washington, also has an employer portion that gets paid along with the employee's portion. So the Department of Labor and Industries designates a rate for a certain type of job, say .50 per hour, and that rate is divided between the employee (.10 per hour) and the employer (.40 per hour). This is paid in at quarterly intervals on a form that reports your total Gross Wages, and the total hours worked which are multiplied by the one rate (employer and employee rates added together). Please check with your state's department for state disability for information on how you are to report for your payroll.

Yikes! Does this mean you have to set up 7 or 8 different payroll tax liability accounts just to keep track of all this??? Well, employees are expensive and complicated no doubt about that. But no, I'll tell you how I like to do this. I set up a main general ledger account in the current liabilities called "Payroll Tax". Under that I have 4 sub accounts: Form 941, Form 940, State Unemployment and State Disability. In the Form

941 account I enter all the employee and employer portions for Social Security and Medicare, and the Federal Withholding. In the Form 940 account I enter all the FUTA. The State Unemployment account is self-explanatory. And I enter both the employee and employer portions into the State Disability account. So, that's easy enough. The real key to all of this, and this is imperative especially if you are doing your payroll manually, is every time you do paychecks for your employees you must make the entries for your Employer portions of payroll tax as well. (If you are using a handy accounting software program, these entries should be made for you as you generate each payroll check.) So based on the example that was way at the beginning of this section, let's see how this looks in "T" accounts:

(Current Liab.)	(Current Liab.)	(Current Liab.)	(Current Liab.)
Soc.Sec. & Med.	FUTA	State Unemp.	State Disability
DR | CR	DR | CR	DR | CR	DR | CR
$38.25	$4.00	$7.50	$6.00

(Expense)

Employer's Payroll Tax

DR | CR

$55.75

So now you see that $55.75 is what it costs you as the employer to generate a $500.00 paycheck. Of course this is speculation, your actual numbers may be different. However, please note that this is the portion that gets logged into your Payroll Tax Expense account as the Debit to balance against all the Credits that are going to be included in your Payroll Tax Liability accounts. The employer portion of these payroll taxes is being expensed. The credit side to each of these transactions, the portions going to the liability accounts, are being "held" in those liability accounts until they come due for payment. Remember, a portion of the amounts being held in the liability accounts is actually your employee's tax money, which you are holding for them until it is time to turn it in. Therefore, please always make sure you have enough cash in your checking account to cover the total of your Payroll Tax Liability accounts. It is your responsibility as an employer to be able to send this money in when it is due. And believe me, these government agencies are quick on the draw and you will save yourself plenty in penalties and interest if you can pay these on time and in full!!

The last form needed by you as an employer for your employees is the W-2 form. This is the form that everyone is hot for right after December 31st so they can send in their tax return and get their refunds! Actually, I try to convince employees that it is really better to break even at the end of the year. Then they get to use their money as they earn it, not giving a free loan to the IRS so they can use the money all year then send a portion of it back. But for some employees, it is the only way they can manage to put money aside, that is the most common response I get.

The W-2 is just a report. You must fill one out for each employee that you have had throughout the year. Even if that employee just took one paycheck you must do a W-2 for each person that was in your employ during the year from Jan.-Dec. no matter how long or short their employment was with you or if they still work for you or not. The W-2 reports to the Social Security Administration the totals for the whole year for each employee's wages, Federal Withholding, Social Security, and Medicare. State withholdings are not reported on this form. However some employee benefits are. Such as certain types of medical plans, and certain employee perks. If you offer any of these to your employees, check with your CPA to make sure this gets reported correctly the first time around. Believe me, redoing W-2's after the fact is a real pain! You would be glad you did it right the first time!

So, let's recap the payroll taxes in an easy to reference list:

Federal Taxes:

Federal Withholding	Reported on Form 941 quarterly	Paid monthly (15th), quarterly, or
	Employee only	per payroll depending on amount.
Social Security & Medicare	Reported on Form 941 quarterly	Paid monthly (15th), quarterly, or
	Employee and Employer portions	per payroll depending on amount.
Federal Unemploy-ment tax	Reported on Form 940 annually	Paid quarterly or annually
	Employer only	depending on amount.

State Taxes:

State Unemployment	Usually reported quarterly	Paid whenever form is due.
	Employer only	Check with your state.
State Disability	Usually reported quarterly	Paid whenever form is due.
	Employee and Employer	Check with your state.
	(Some states).	

This is the best information I can give you regarding your payroll responsibilities as an employer. If you get really confused regarding rates, reporting times, filling out the forms, etc... please don't hesitate to call the related government agency or look up their website. This is where I had received a lot of my information when I was first starting out. They are always helpful and always willing to set you straight on your information. And most of them are always friendly too!

Inventory

If you have a business that has inventory on hand (parts, shop items for sale, etc...), then keeping inventory is a really good tool. What this means is taking an accurate count of your stocked goods on a regular basis. Some businesses like to do it monthly, quarterly, or even yearly. A restaurant I work with likes to do it weekly. It helps them with ordering and planning, most obviously. Also this way they can keep track of wine bottles walking out the door with late night employees! It happens! So whatever your needs are should dictate how often it would be necessary for you to do this task. Some examples of businesses that have a stocked inventory are: restaurants, retail stores, job shops such as auto or marine repairs or manufacturing, any business that buys inventory up front to be resold or used in assembling a product to be sold. This is just to give you an idea. If you are a contractor of some sort and only buy parts or materials for use on individual jobs, this doesn't apply to your business. Your purchases simply get recorded under your "Cost of Goods Sold" expense account. Also, if you sell items taken on "consignment" these items are <u>not</u> recognized as inventory and do not need to be counted. Consider if you even need to spend time on this chapter or not! One thing for certain is every business with stocked goods does need to take an accurate inventory count at least by the end of December if they do it only once during the year.

For instance, have you ever wondered why so many retail stores have giant year-end sales? This is specifically to **reduce** their inventory. The less inventory they have on hand on December 31st, the better it is for the business's tax picture. Here is the reason for that: The IRS needs a figure at the end of the year for "cost of goods sold". The way it is figured for tax purposes is to take the starting inventory as of Jan. 1st, add all the purchases made that add to the inventory throughout the year, plus any labor costs (the owner excluded), plus any materials or supplies relating to the business. From this sum we **subtract** the inventory count on Dec. 31st and the result is the figure used by the IRS as "cost of goods sold" which is then a <u>deduction</u> against the income of the business.

It would look like this: (say you just started your business this year and it's a manufacturing shop).

Beginning inventory Jan. 1st =	0.00
Purchases to add inventory	= 2,500.00
Assembly worker wages	= 10,500.00
Shop supplies	= 1,000.00
Sub-total	= 14,000.00
Minus year end inventory	= 1,500.00
Total cost of goods sold for tax purposes.	= 12,500.00

Wow! A deduction of $12,500.00 from your income figure can save you a lot in taxes. Of course this is an ideal situation but you can get the idea now.

So after you have decided that yours is a business that does keep stocked goods on hand and those goods are regarded and treated as your business's inventory, how do you make the entries to record your purchases and sales, and your cost versus your marked up price?? Well, this can be done a couple of different ways depending on what type of business you have, how you are going to keep track of your inventory and what you are using as a way of doing your bookkeeping (a computer program or manually). Essentially, the correct way to do it accounting-wise, (and what a computer program will do for you automatically if you have it set up that way), is as follows:

(Here is how it looks in "T Accounts". Remember "T Accounts" are graphic pictures you can draw of what your accounting entries look like either as you enter them into a manual system or to help you follow along with your computer.)

	Inventory Asset			Checking	
DR		CR	DR		CR
$500.00 (your cost)					$500.00 (your cost)

When you make a purchase to add to your inventory the "debit" side of the entry goes into your "Inventory **Asset**" account. The "credit" side is to your checking account if you just simply wrote a check for the items, or to your accounts payable if you are recording the purchase and planning to make a payment for it at a later date. The amount you are recording in this transaction is your cost of the items, not what you will be reselling them for. As a point of fact, the only amounts recorded in your Inventory Asset account are your costs. And, to re-cap our previous information, your Inventory Asset account is called this because it is an Asset account, which is a debit account, and is an account that makes up your total asset picture on your Balance Sheet.

That was the easy part. Now when you sell the goods, there are a couple of transactions that need to take place. The first part is when you sell an item; your cost is entered as a "credit" to your Inventory Asset account and a "debit" to your Cost of Goods Sold expense account. This is how you get the cost of your inventory out of your assets, because they are now sold, and into your expenses. Because once you have sold an item out of your inventory it then ceases to be an asset (hanging around indefinitely in your storage room or shop), and becomes an actual expense (as it goes out the door with your customer).

	Inventory Asset			Cost of Goods Sold	
DR		CR	DR		CR
	(your cost)	$500.00	$500.00 (your cost)		

The last part of this transaction is recording the sale itself. And the sale is recorded in just the usual way with the "credit" side being recorded to your sales and the "debit" side being recorded either as a deposit to your checking account or into your accounts receivable if you have billed your customer for the goods and they will pay you at a later date. Please note that now is the time you are recording the marked up price for your items. That is the amount for which you are reselling your items to your customers.

	Sales (Income)			Checking	
DR			CR	DR			CR
(marked up price)	$650.00		$650.00	(marked up price)

So you see you can be as detailed and meticulous as you want to be regarding your inventory. In my wide range of customers, I have seen them all choose different styles of keeping track of inventory. I'll give you some examples:

One retail shop I work with takes inventory only once a year at the end of December. And each month we make an adjustment based on the average mark up of the items for sale to move the inventory sold from the Inventory Asset account to the Cost of Goods Sold expense account. So every time this store purchases inventory for resale we debit the Inventory Asset account. And some items are sold for 25% more than purchased some are sold for 30% more. We take the sales figures from each month and multiply the two sales categories by their respective percentage rates and that is the amount we move from the Inventory Assets to the Cost of Goods Sold. Then at the end of the year when they do their actual inventory count, if the actual count is different from what is in the Inventory Asset account, then we make an adjustment against the Cost of Goods Sold expense account to match the Inventory Asset account to the actual count that was taken. One reason we do this is because the sales out of this store are all done manually. In other words, the sales are not recorded electronically at the point of sale. So it would not be practical to keep track of the individual items sold on a daily basis, and then make all the individual entries, etc... it would be more time consuming than it is worth. These days there is a lot of "point of sale" software available that would allow each sale to be recorded electronically. This type of software can be good for a retail store, as it will keep track of your inventory for you automatically as you sell each item, provided, of course, you entered the items as you purchased them in the first place.

I also work with a coffee company. This is technically a manufacturing company. And this company does work their inventory based on the true accounting principles as I explained above. This is for a couple reasons. One is we use a good accounting software program that does all these transactions automatically. ☺ Another is because it is practical to do so. We are only dealing with one product, coffee beans. They are all purchased for basically the same price and, once roasted, they are all sold for basically the same price. Then once every quarter we take an accurate physical inventory count and match up the Inventory Asset account against the actual count and make our adjustment against the Cost of Goods Sold expense account if necessary at that time.

The restaurant I mentioned at the top of this chapter does their inventory weekly. Of course they need to because their product moves in and out very quickly on a daily basis. This greatly helps them with their planning and purchasing and keeping their food costs down. But for this we use a spreadsheet that has all the items kept in stock at the time, (some of it is seasonal), with all their current costs listed. And we just simply put in the current count, multiply out the values using the current costs and get a total. This is a great tool for them and they are a very successful restaurant. I believe it is a direct result of the owners being so involved with the financial goings on of the business.

So you see these few case histories. I hope from this chapter you can decide if one of these methods is right for you. If you are a business that keeps stocked goods, I think you will notice a good tightening up of your cash flow once you start applying a close and consistent method of inventory tracking.

Bank Reconciliation

There are so many people in business who don't know how to reconcile their checking accounts to their bank statements. If you are one of these, you are not alone, trust me. But it is a very important function if you want to stay on top of your checking account balance. If you are like most small businesses, your checking account is one of your main cash sources. So to save yourself lots of extra fees, and maybe some bounced checks, reconcile your checking account to your bank statement once a month and you will be glad you did. And, whether you use an accounting program on your computer, or you are doing it manually, it all gets done the same way. So here is what to do:

With your bank statement open right next to your check register, start checking off the things that appear both in your bank statement and your check register. This would include any deposits made, checks written, and either deposits or deductions made to your account by your bank that you have also noted in your check register prior to receiving your statement. (Sometimes your bank does send you little slips of paper advising you that they have done this. Take advantage of these slips of paper by writing the adjustment into your check register when you receive them.) This is also a great way to discover any deposits you made or checks you wrote but neglected to put them into your checking account balance. By going through this exercise, you also may discover any errors made by your bank!

After checking off all your deposits and checks, you will then need to choose a date through which you are reconciling your checking account. For most businesses this is simply the last day of the month for which you are reconciling. However there are some businesses that receive their bank statements with a cutoff date of somewhere in the middle of the month. If your business is set up like this with your bank, it is OK to use the same date your bank statement uses for the "ending date". You won't gain anything but extra work for yourself by using the last day of the month in this situation.

Now the next step is to make a list of all the checks and deposits that you have made **up through** the ending date you have chosen that do **NOT** appear on your bank statement. This is why the ending date is important. The date you choose does not affect anything but how many extra checks and deposits you must list that do not appear on your bank statement. It has been my experience that the more of these you have to list, the more chances there are for mistakes to be made in this area. By using the ending date as noted on your bank statement, you will definitely shorten this list if their cut off for you is in the middle of the month.

This is where I want to make a couple notes to you:

1. You will be doing yourself a great favor if you enter all checks and deposits into your check register as they are made. Regardless of whether your bank says your checks have cleared or not, you should **always** count your checks written as being **absent** from your balance. This way if someone hangs on to a check for a little extra time, it won't come as a shock to you when that check finally does clear your account. (Those of you who operate this way know what I am talking about!)

2. If you are one of those businesses whose bank has your ending date in the middle of the month, you may want to ask them to change that date to the last day of the month. Do this only if you are struggling with the date they have chosen. A bank will switch your ending date to the one you desire, but to do this, of course, they will charge you. However, it is possible.

So, now you have checked off all the checks and deposits that appear in your check register and on your bank statement. You have made a listing of all the checks and deposits that do not appear on your bank statement up through the ending date you are working with. Here is how it all fits together:

There are two sides to deal with now. The bank's side and your check register's side. On the bank's side start off with **their ending balance** as usually shown on the front of your bank statement. Take that list you made of all the checks and deposits that do **not** appear on your bank statement. To the bank's ending balance add the deposits you have made but did not clear as of your statement date, and subtract all the checks you have listed that have not cleared as of your statement date. Hold onto this figure for a minute. Now on your check register's side start off with the balance showing in your check register that is on the same date as you have chosen for your ending date. To your ending balance add any deposits your bank has made to your account, (such as an interest payment), and subtract any deductions your bank has made to your account, (such as bank fees or service charges), provided, of course, you have not already included such transactions prior to your ending date. This figure should be **exactly** the same as the end result that you arrived at for the bank's side of this exercise. If it is, congratulations! You are done. Was that hard? After you do it several months in a row, it will get easier and easier.

- **Note:** If you haven't already entered any interest payments or service charges into your check register prior to discovering them on your bank statement, you will want to put them in your register now. If you enter these into your check register after you have reconciled your account, no matter what date you enter them on, go ahead and put check marks by them because you won't be dealing with them again. The check marks in your register indicate transactions that have already cleared your bank account and will not be showing themselves again.

Now, what happens if the figure you come up with on the bank's side and the figure you get on your check register's side is **not exactly the same?** Well, this means you have some detective work to do. I have a list of problem solving items that I go through to seek out the discrepancy in the unbalanced check register. Starting with the easiest and most obvious errors first here is the list:

1. Did you pick the correct ending balance out of the check register? Check the date of the ending balance, if incorrect, use the correct one.
2. Is the math correct in the check register? Using a good calculator, go back to the last known reconciled balance and start adding and subtracting till you come up to your newly chosen ending balance. (You may want to run a paper "tape" on the calculator.) Maybe it's a math error.

44

3. Figure out the difference between the two ending figures from the bank's side and the check register's side. Can you divide it by two? If you can, it is an indication that a check got entered as a deposit or a deposit got entered as a check. (A little math trick). Go back through your check register and see if something got into the wrong column and correct the entry. If you can't divide the difference by two....

4. Go back through the comparison process again. Matching check for check, deposit for deposit. Did you record the correct amount of the check or deposit in your register? Did you skip over a check or deposit in your register? Maybe it is one that never got listed to your register. Or maybe there is a check or deposit that should be on your "transactions NOT cleared" list. If you start all over at the beginning and go through this process again you are almost certain to find the error here, if the first 3 steps turned up nothing. If the error is STILL unsolved and you have tried all these things...

5. This is my favorite: Guess what? It might be an error made by the bank! Yes, they do make errors. Some banks make more errors than others! If you are constantly finding errors made by your bank you may want to switch banks. One way to seek out a bank error that isn't obvious is to check the magnetic encoding on your returned checks. (Note: this only works if your bank returns your cancelled checks to you with your statement.) Look at the cancelled checks returned to you by your bank with your statement. In the bottom right corner on the front of your check is a number that represents what the bank cleared your check for. Check to make certain that the encoded number matches the dollar amount shown on your check. If these two don't match, and I have run across this situation several times, the bank may have used your correct dollar amount on your statement but when the check ran through their system they picked up the incorrect encoded amount. See? Then your ending balance is actually appearing incorrectly on your statement. At this point you will probably have to make a trip to your bank with the cancelled check in question, and your statement and they will have to adjust their records accordingly. But for the purpose of finishing the task at hand, take the difference between the amount you wrote your check for and the encoded amount and see if this is the amount you are off.

If you are still having trouble getting your check register and your bank to match, you can always take the whole thing to your bank and ask them for help. Most banks usually have a sympathetic someone who helps with things of this nature. But be warned, it has been my experience that this generally only serves to confuse the situation more. However, on a positive note, I am certain that if you go through the process of the steps listed above, you will have great success in balancing your checking account to your bank statement! Try it out. I know you will be glad you did.

Choosing Bookkeeping Software

This isn't as easy as it sounds. There are literally hundreds of choices out there. If you have come to the point where you are comfortable entering your bookkeeping information and you want to be more automated than just using a notebook or columnar pad then you have to make this choice. I am hesitant to make any solid recommendations here. I've found over the years that people's tastes vary in software as much as in any other area where there are a lot of choices. Plus you have to consider what the right choice for your business is as well. But I can tell you what I've used in the past.

I mostly use various forms of Quickbooks in a lot of the small businesses I work with. For me this is easy to teach to someone and it is also friendly enough if bookkeeping and accounting are not in the forefront of your thinking.

I know someone who uses Quicken for her business. This I can tell you I would not recommend. Quicken is very good to use for your home and household bookkeeping. But this was not designed for business use. And if you try to get any useful reports out of it, for instance, you will see why. So don't mix these two up! Quickbooks is for business, Quicken is for your household.

These days Quickbooks comes in many forms too. So depending on the nature of your business you may find one of the Quickbooks formats is going to work for you. They even make point of sale versions now as well as versions for contractors. These all have their variances which make them unique for the industries they are designed for. So research this before making a choice. Quickbooks is made by Intuit.

I have worked with good bookkeeping software called Peachtree. Peachtree was one of the very first bookkeeping software ever developed. It first came up in the early 80's I believe. It is a bit more sophisticated than Quickbooks as far as reporting goes for one example. But it also is easier to use if you do have some bookkeeping background or if you are very comfortable with the bookkeeping duties your business will require from you.

Cougar Mountain puts out some good modular software. Whereas products like Quickbooks and Peachtree are inclusive of everything you would need for any scenario that would come up for your small business, the Cougar Mountain products allow you to purchase whatever modules you will need. You could purchase just a Payroll module, or one for Inventory and Point of Sale as an example. So you could build your bookkeeping software this way.

The most sophisticated accounting software I have worked with lately is called MAS-90 made by Sage. This is also modular software. This is good if you will be doing a lot of selling online. Not a home based EBay business for instance. But if you manufacture a product and have a warehouse full of inventory and you will be hiring people to process orders for you, and you will have a shipping department that needs to be linked to the rest of the office. That kind of business. This might be software worth researching.

And for every company I've just mentioned there are at least a ton more in each style I've mentioned too! Lots of modular software, lots of all inclusive software, really sophisticated programs, really simple programs. You must be prepared to research. Ask your business peers what software they use. And if you think you settle on one brand over another, hunt down someone who uses it and pick their brain!!

Go on the internet and read blogs. A couple of good websites for researching this very subject are FindAccountingSoftware.com and InternetBasedMoms.com.

Seek out and read product reviews, especially if a software comes out with a different version frequently. One of the good and bad things about bookkeeping software is they are always being updated. This is good, I suppose. But it is really sad to learn a version of your favorite software really well and you come to like it and recommend it to your friends. Then the next year they come out with a new version and find a way to force you to upgrade and the upgrade is way more convoluted and expensive than the version you were just using. And it's filled with unnecessary graphics now that your 3 year old computer has a slow time processing. And graphic interfaces you were used to seeing have all changed, and the once friendly program now seems strange and unfriendly. Oh yes, this happens! So it is good to find out as much as you can before you lock into one brand of software over another.

Keep in mind you will want to choose one brand that you will want to stick with over the years. This is because as your company gains financial history and it is all in the format of one bookkeeping program it will get harder and harder to switch programs and be able to take your company's financial history with you into the new program.

So much to think about! Makes me wish we all could still get along with just our pencils, calculators and columnar journals! I'll tell you this sometimes I feel like those days were a lot easier! So much for high tech.

THE END

Well, this is the end of all you need to know to get things started off in the right direction. I sincerely hope you have found this easy to read and follow along with. Remember, if you need help with anything at all, go directly to the source and ask questions! You will find most governmental agencies, banks, and other institutions pertinent to your business, very easy to get answers from if you just call and ask. It helps them as well if your business structure and bookkeeping system is set up correctly. You may run into that old thing where "if you ask 3 different people the same question you will get 3 different answers". My suggestion to you, and what I have done for myself, is to just keep persevering. And, if you need a helping hand, please get in touch with your local independent bookkeeper. In doing so you will be making a valuable contact. I wish you many happy and stress free years in your business adventure!

NOTES

NOTES

NOTES

NOTES

Made in the USA
Lexington, KY
18 April 2010